WILD BOARS

BY LIBBY WILSON

Apex is distributed by North Star Editions:
sales@northstareditions.com | 888-417-0195

Produced for Apex by Red Line Editorial.

Photographs ©: Shutterstock Images, cover, 1, 4–5, 6–7, 8, 9, 10–11, 12–13, 15, 16–17, 18, 19, 22–23, 24, 26–27; iStockphoto, 14; Gregorio Borgia/AP Images, 20, 29

Library of Congress Control Number: 2022910616

ISBN
978-1-63738-445-9 (hardcover)
978-1-63738-472-5 (paperback)
978-1-63738-523-4 (ebook pdf)
978-1-63738-499-2 (hosted ebook)

Printed in the United States of America
Mankato, MN
012023

NOTE TO PARENTS AND EDUCATORS

Apex books are designed to build literacy skills in striving readers. Exciting, high-interest content attracts and holds readers' attention. The text is carefully leveled to allow students to achieve success quickly. Additional features, such as bolded glossary words for difficult terms, help build comprehension.

TABLE OF CONTENTS

CHAPTER 1

PIGGING out

Thirty hungry wild boars trot into a field after dark. Their **snouts** dig like shovels. They gobble up roots, grass, and earthworms.

Wild boars look for food buried in dirt or leaves.

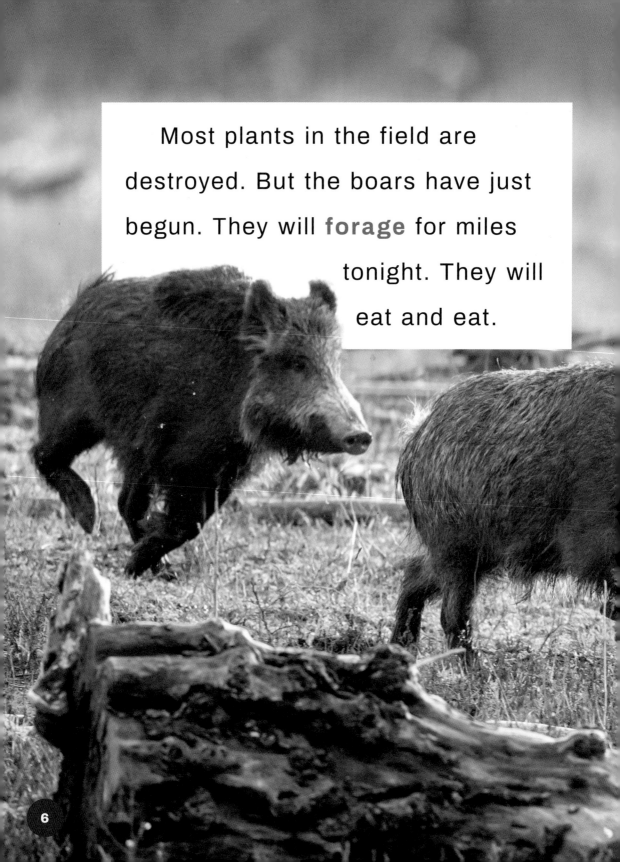

Most plants in the field are destroyed. But the boars have just begun. They will **forage** for miles tonight. They will eat and eat.

EATING IT ALL

Wild boars are omnivores. They mainly eat plants. But their diet also includes insects, nuts, birds, and snakes. Sometimes they even eat newborn animals.

Boars can travel between 5 and 20 miles (8 and 32 km) to find food.

Boars can leave behind holes that are more than 3 feet (0.9 m) deep.

Morning dawns. The boars take cover in bushes or woods. They leave behind fields with huge holes and mounds of dirt. It's time for the boars to sleep.

In summer, wild boars are mostly **nocturnal**. They avoid the daytime heat.

When it is cool and safe, wild boars sometimes forage during daylight hours.

CHAPTER 2

RUNNING WILD

Wild boars are pigs. All pigs are **native** to Europe and Asia. Settlers brought them to the Americas. Some pigs ran free. They grew **feral**. These pigs are called wild boars.

Wild boars live in more than 50 countries around the world.

Boars have large, strong bodies. They can weigh up to 800 pounds (363 kg).

Wild boars have strong muscles in their necks and shoulders.

FAST FACT

Despite their size, wild boars are fast. They can run 30 miles per hour (48 km/h).

A male boar's tusks keep growing throughout its whole life.

Four sharp tusks jut out from boars' jaws. These teeth can grow 5 inches (13 cm) long. Boars use them to fight and dig up plants. Boars also use their tusks to mark their **territory**.

WARNING SMELL

Boars have a strong sense of smell. A boar sometimes rubs its face against trees. That leaves a scent. The scent tells the other boars to stay away.

Male wild boars might fight over food or females.

CHAPTER 3

AROUND THE WORLD

Boars can thrive wherever there is water. They are found near swamps and marshes. They live in forests and grasslands, too.

Boars sometimes use water to cool off.
They are good swimmers.

Most boars live in warm places. But they can also adapt to cold climates. They dig dens. Boars line the dens with plants to keep warm.

Food is harder to find in winter. Boars often eat roots buried under snow.

Female boars and their babies often live in groups of 6 to 20.

SHARING SPACES

Male boars may live alone. But females often form groups. Females have babies in shallow nests. Then they join other females and piglets. They share dens and water holes.

Wild boars can even live near people. As people destroy natural areas, some boars learn to live in cities. They eat trash at night. They uproot plants.

FAST FACT

Boars hide from people when possible. But they may attack if **threatened**.

Boars sometimes cross the street right in front of cars.

CHAPTER 4

BOAR PROBLEMS

Boars do have some **predators**, including bears and wolves. But most predators don't eat wild boars very often. As a result, the number of boars can rise quickly.

If predators like wolves don't eat enough wild boars, the number of wild boars will keep going up.

Some places have too many wild boars. These boars cause many problems. They can kill plants in lawns and fields. And they can spread diseases.

BIG BAD BOARS

Boars often eat food that native animals need. Those animals may die out. Boars can be dangerous for people, too. Cars or other vehicles may crash into them.

◀ Wild boars often eat or damage crops that people grow for food.

So, people work to limit boars'
numbers. Some people hunt boars.
Others keep them from spreading to
new areas.

People should stay away if they see a pack of boars.

FAST FACT

Wild boars are very smart, so they are hard to trap.

COMPREHENSION
QUESTIONS

Write your answers on a separate piece of paper.

1. Write a few sentences describing some of the problems wild boars can cause.

2. Do you think hunting is a good way to limit the number of some animals? Why or why not?

3. Why are wild boars moving into cities?

    A. Boars try to live as close to humans as possible.

    B. People are destroying the places where boars used to live.

    C. Cities are warmer than the places where boars used to live.

4. Why do boars take cover during the day?

    A. because people are chasing them

    B. so they can find more food

    C. to find a safe place to sleep

5. What does **adapt** mean in this book?

Most boars live in warm places. But they can also adapt to cold climates.

    A. stay exactly the same

    B. change to live in a new place

    C. learn how to grow more food

6. What does **dangerous** mean in this book?

Boars can be dangerous for people, too. Cars or other vehicles may crash into them.

    A. causing harm

    B. bringing peace

    C. giving money

Answer key on page 32.

GLOSSARY

feral
Wild.

forage
To search for food.

native
Originally living in an area.

nocturnal
Awake and active at night.

omnivores
Animals that eat both plants and animals.

predators
Animals that hunt and eat other animals.

snouts
The noses and mouths of animals.

territory
An area that an animal or group of animals lives in and defends.

threatened
Put in danger.

BOOKS

Duling, Kaitlyn. *Wild Yaks*. Minneapolis: Bellwether Media, 2021.

Reynolds, Donna. *Wild Boars in the Forest.* New York: Gareth Stevens Publishing, 2023.

Sabelko, Rebecca. *Wild Turkeys*. Minneapolis: Bellwether Media, 2019.

ONLINE RESOURCES

Visit **www.apexeditions.com** to find links and resources related to this title.

ABOUT THE AUTHOR

Libby Wilson is a retired librarian. She loves to research and learn amazing facts about nature to share with readers. Ms. Wilson lives in Pennsylvania and North Carolina with her husband and golden retriever.

INDEX

ANSWER KEY:
1. Answers will vary; 2. Answers will vary; 3. B; 4. C; 5. B; 6. A